SCIENCE AND TECHNOLOGY
START-UP STARS

INDUSTRY Entrepreneurs

James Bow

CRABTREE
PUBLISHING COMPANY
WWW.CRABTREEBOOKS.COM

CRABTREE
PUBLISHING COMPANY
WWW.CRABTREEBOOKS.COM

Author: James Bow

Editors: Sarah Eason, Nancy Dickmann, Wendy Scavuzzo, and Petrice Custance

Proofreader and indexer: Wendy Scavuzzo

Editorial director: Kathy Middleton

Design: Clare Webber

Cover design and additional artwork: Clare Webber

Photo research: Rachel Blount

Production coordinator and Prepress technician: Tammy McGarr

Print coordinator: Katherine Berti

Consultant: David Hawksett

Produced for Crabtree Publishing Company by Calcium Creative

Photo Credits:

t=Top, tr=Top Right, tl=Top Left

Inside: 3D Hubs (www.3dhubs.com): pp. 12, 13t; © Classic Factory Switzerland: p. 6; Roshanda Cummings: p. 20; Flickr: Creative Tools: p. 13b; Anne-Marie Imafidon: p. 23b; Kevin Lee: p. 17; Pixabay: Sasint: p. 28; Shutterstock: AlesiaKan: p. 27; Alex_Traksel: p. 11t; Grzegorz Czapski: p. 7t; Orange Deer: p. 15t; DONOT6_STUDIO: p. 18; Gorodenkoff: pp. 1, 16; Kathy Hutchins: p. 5b; Morphart Creation: p. 5t; MrNovel: p. 19t; NadyaEugene: p. 16; Syda Productions: pp. 3, 11b; SunFarmer: Brendan P. Davis: p. 19b; Wikimedia Commons: DARPA: p. 22; Sgt. Sarah Dietz, U.S. Marine Corps: p. 24; Hodlipson: p. 10; Joi Ito from Inbamura, Japan: p. 23t; Steve Jurvetson: p. 9m; Jusdafax: p. 29; Kuebi = Armin Kübelbeck: p. 21; Maurizio Pesce: p. 8; © Ralf Roletschek: p. 14; SpaceX: p. 9t; TechCrunch: p. 25; Ubahnverleih: p. 15b; Dmitry Valber: p. 4.

Cover: Shutterstock: Pressmaster.

Library and Archives Canada Cataloguing in Publication

Bow, James, 1972-, author
Industry entrepreneurs / James Bow.

(Science and technology start-up stars)
Includes index.
Issued in print and electronic formats.
ISBN 978-0-7787-4420-7 (hardcover).--
ISBN 978-0-7787-4426-9 (softcover).--
ISBN 978-1-4271-2024-3 (HTML)

1. Technological innovations--Juvenile literature. 2. Entrepreneurship--uvenile literature. I. Title.

T173.8.B695 2018 j303.48′3 C2017-907658-2
C2017-907659-0

Library of Congress Cataloging-in-Publication Data

CIP available at the Library of Congress

Crabtree Publishing Company
www.crabtreebooks.com 1-800-387-7650

Printed in the U.S.A./022018/CG20171220

Published in Canada
Crabtree Publishing
616 Welland Ave.
St. Catharines, Ontario
L2M 5V6

Published in the United States
Crabtree Publishing
PMB 59051
350 Fifth Avenue, 59th Floor
New York, New York 10118

Published in the United Kingdom
Crabtree Publishing
Maritime House
Basin Road North, Hove
BN41 1WR

Published in Australia
Crabtree Publishing
3 Charles Street
Coburg North
VIC, 3058

CONTENTS

You Can Be an Entrepreneur! 4
The New Car Companies 6
Electric Car Start-Up Star: Elon Musk 8
Home Factories 10
3-D Start-Up Stars: Bram de Zwart and Brian Garrett 12
Tiny Technology 14
Nanotech Start-Up Star: Rachel Pautler 16
We Have the Power! 18
Electric Start-Up Star: Elena Foukes Lucas 20
Computers and Robots 22
Robotic Start-Up Star: Marc Raibert 24
Entrepreneurs Changing the World 26
Your Start-Up Story 28
Glossary 30
Learning More 31
Index 32

YOU CAN BE AN ENTREPRENEUR!

In July 2017, a crowd gathered outside a **factory** in Fremont, California. They were there to watch **entrepreneur** Elon Musk reveal the Tesla Model 3—an **electric car** that could travel 220 miles (354 km) when fully charged. Musk had begun Tesla Motors in 2003, when he was 32 years old. The Tesla was the fulfillment of his dream to change the car **industry** by making electric cars just as capable as gasoline-burning vehicles. His achievement is a great example of how young entrepreneurs can use science and technology to build a business that can change the world.

ENTREPRENEURS AND START-UPS

An entrepreneur is someone who plans, starts, and runs a business that provides **goods** or **services**. Entrepreneurs are people who take risks to develop new products and start new businesses. They have an original or **innovative** idea. They then turn it into a business that supplies those goods or services. Start-ups are new businesses created by entrepreneurs.

ENTREPRENEURS CHANGING THE WORLD

An industry is a large group of businesses and economic activities, such as buying and selling. Industries make goods or provide services. For example, the car industry makes and sells cars. The world is changing at a fast pace. As new technologies are introduced, industries adopt the technologies. The world also faces challenges, such as pollution and finding energy sources. Entrepreneurs in different industries are using their skills to tackle these challenges and make a better world.

Tesla hopes to make its electric cars as fast, reliable, and affordable as regular cars.

INSPIRING STORIES

Early Thinkers

Young science and technology entrepreneurs have been around since the **Industrial Revolution**! Before the beginning of the 1800s, most people in Europe and North America were farmers. Then the discovery of **steam power** made big machines and factories possible. English inventor George Stephenson realized he could use a steam engine to move people and goods. At the age of just 33, he created a start-up business and built the first steam **locomotive**. His invention helped create modern trains, which brought food to cities and coal to factories. This forever changed the way people lived and worked.

The first locomotives traveled slowly, but inventors kept experimenting and improving.

ENTREPRENEURS OF THE FUTURE

New technologies are changing our world at an incredible pace, and young people just like you could be the science and technology entrepreneurs of tomorrow. Perhaps you and your friends will follow in the footsteps of stars such as Stephenson and Musk, and go on to create exciting start-ups of your own!

Elon Musk pays himself a salary of just $1 per year to be **CEO** of Tesla Motors. He makes money by owning Tesla stock, which goes up in value if the company is successful.

THE NEW CAR COMPANIES

From the beginning of the 1900s, large car **manufacturing** companies have made billions of dollars and employed thousands of people. Companies such as Ford, Chrysler, and Nissan have worked hard to make sure their cars do not waste **fuel**. However, the cars still burn **fossil fuels** such as gasoline. Fossil fuels are harmful to the environment. Transportation in the United States is responsible for more than one-quarter of the country's **greenhouse gas emissions**. These trap heat in Earth's atmosphere, which contributes to **global warming**. However, small start-up companies are developing new technologies to make cars that do not use fossil fuels. Some smart young entrepreneurs have set up new car companies to do just that.

The Elextra, a luxury electric car designed by the Swiss company Classic Factory, can accelerate to 62 mph (99 kph) in just 2.3 seconds.

The Chinese company Great Wall Motors has unveiled the WEY hybrid car, which combines a gas engine with a plug-in battery.

ON THE SHOULDERS OF GIANTS

Electric motors may have been around longer than gasoline-powered engines, but successful entrepreneurs know how to give old ideas a new twist! This can be seen in the work of entrepreneur Elon Musk. Way back in 1882, the inventor Nikola Tesla (1856–1943) designed an electrical motor. Fast-forward to 2008, and Musk used Tesla's motor design to power his own first electric car, the Tesla Roadster. Musk named his company Tesla Motors, after the brilliant inventor.

INSPIRING OTHERS

Tesla's cars have excited people. From 2018, the company expects to sell more than 500,000 cars each year. This has inspired other young start-up entrepreneurs to set up their own electric car companies, hoping to compete with Tesla Motors. For example, in China, former Volvo executive Freeman Shen set up a start-up business called WM Motors and raised a billion dollars to build his own brand of electric vehicles.

INSPIRING STORIES

Super Solar Power

Since 1988, students and professors at the University of Waterloo, in Ontario, Canada, have been working on Midnight Sun. This is a **solar-powered** vehicle designed to compete in races around the world. Eleven models of Midnight Sun have competed in races such as the Australia Solar Challenge. The University of Waterloo team tests new ideas on each version. They hope that this will help people learn more about renewable energy. They also hope to help young entrepreneurs explore more ideas for using solar power.

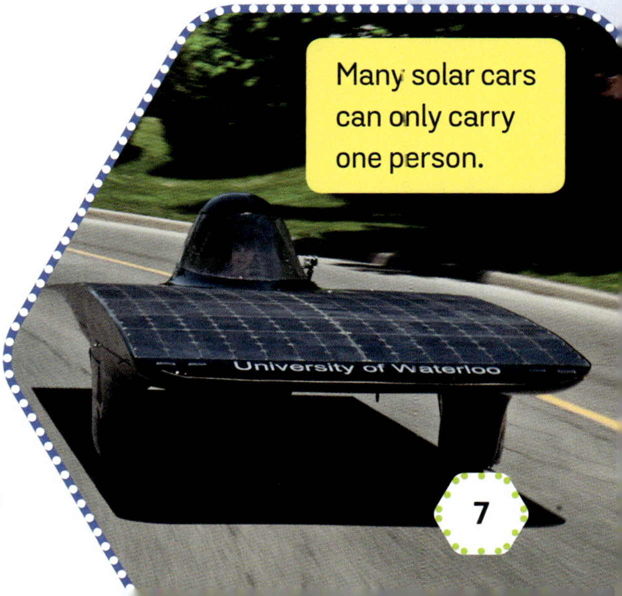

Many solar cars can only carry one person.

ELECTRIC CAR START-UP STAR: ELON MUSK

Elon Musk was born in South Africa in 1971. At a young age, Musk taught himself to program computers. He even invented a video game called Blastar at just 12 years old. Musk showed early entrepreneurial skills by selling the game's code to the computer magazine *PC and Office Technology*! He went on to study at Queen's University in Kingston, Ontario, the University of Pennsylvania, and Stanford University in California. During his Ph.D. studies at Stanford, he decided to leave to start his own business.

Musk's first businesses were in helping people transfer money over the Internet. He set up Zip2, then X.com, and finally PayPal, which was eventually sold to eBay for $1.5 billion. Musk **invested** his share of the sale into other business ideas that could help solve world issues such as pollution. These include Tesla Motors. In his words, "Going from PayPal, I thought: 'Well, what are some of the other problems that are likely to most affect the future of humanity?' Not from the perspective, 'What's the best way to make money?'"

Elon Musk sold his first company, Zip2, in 1999 for $307 million.

INTO SPACE!

Elon Musk is full of ideas that may change the world for the better. In 2002, he set up the company SpaceX to increase the number of flights into space, to launch **satellites**, and to encourage **space tourism**. He has suggested launching satellites in low **orbit** around the world to create a Wi-Fi **network** to bring the Internet to **remote** areas.

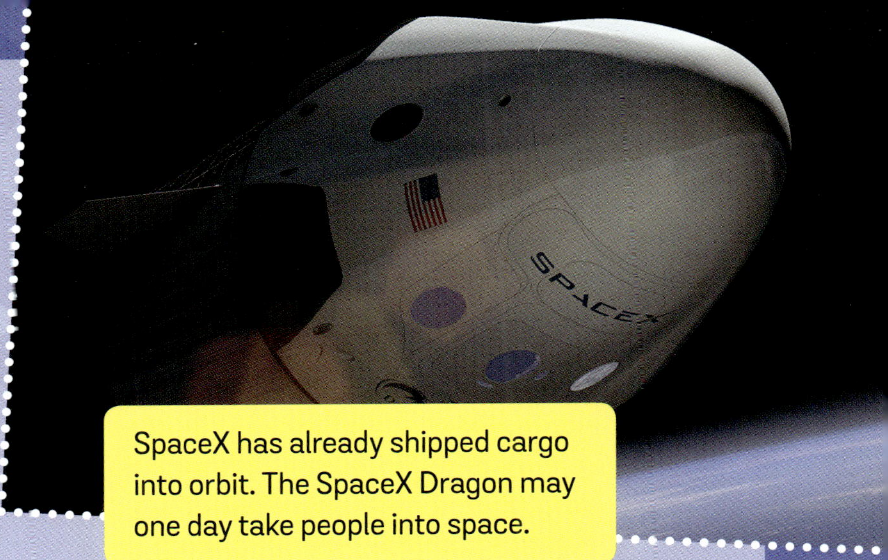

SpaceX has already shipped cargo into orbit. The SpaceX Dragon may one day take people into space.

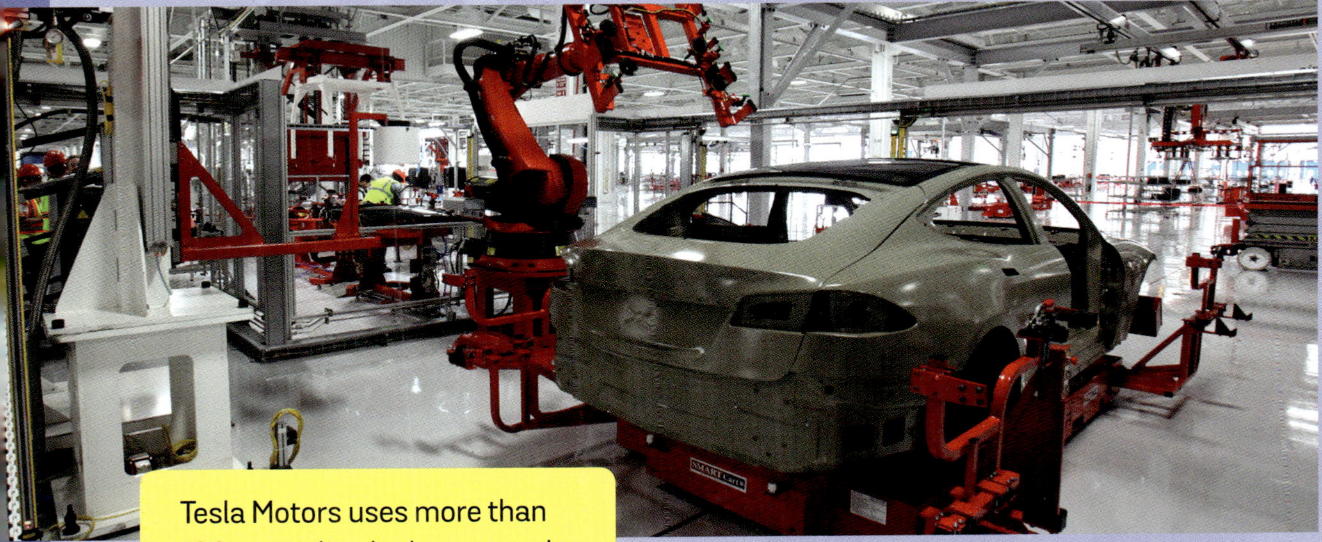

Tesla Motors uses more than 160 specialized robots to make its cars. These include ten of the largest robots in the world.

SOLAR POWER AND SELF-DRIVING CARS

In 2017, Tesla Motors created roof **shingles** that collect solar energy. The company also made a battery wall that can store solar power for use when the Sun is not shining. Tesla is also researching self-driving cars.

HYPER TRAINS

In 2013, Musk proposed the idea of the Hyperloop. These are high-speed trains that hover over magnetic tracks. The trains move through tubes in which most of the air has been removed to reduce **air resistance**. The electric trains do not burn fossil fuels and would allow people to travel at very high speeds. Musk is allowing other entrepreneurs to help develop the idea. These start-up stars are testing concepts, perfecting technology, and hoping to bring Musk's idea to people everywhere.

HOME FACTORIES

Industrial machines have allowed us to make cars, goods, clothing, and other items cheaply. However, the machines are usually very large, and companies need large factories to operate them. Thanks to computers and new materials, today the machines that make things are much smaller. With the invention of 3-D printers and **computer-aided designs**, items can be printed in machines that are small enough to fit on your desk!

3-D BREAKTHROUGH

One of the breakthroughs that made 3-D printing possible came thanks to Chuck Hull. In 1983, Hull discovered photopolymers, which are plastics that harden quickly under **ultraviolet (UV) light**. Plastic can be melted and shaped, but without discovering a way to harden it quickly, 3-D printers would have remained big, bulky machines. In 1986, Hull set up his company, 3D Systems, to sell and improve his photopolymer technology. Today, the company has grown to more than 2,000 employees. It sells 3-D printers, scanners, and **software**.

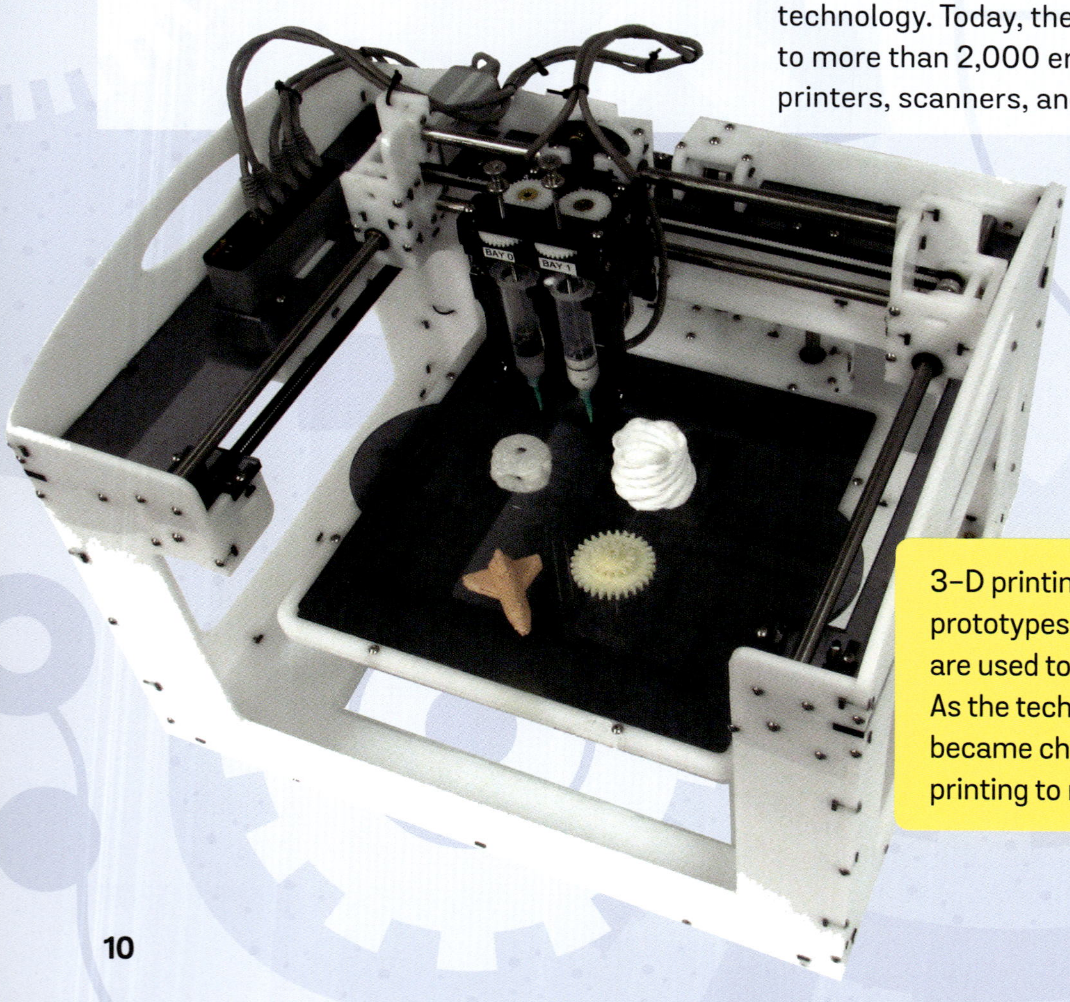

3-D printing was first used to build prototypes. These are models that are used to make finished pieces. As the technology improved and became cheaper, people used 3-D printing to make the finished goods.

Some 3-D printers come as kits, with parts that can be printed from other 3-D printers.

MAKE IT AT HOME!

Today, 3-D printers also work by carving wood, or by cutting or shaping metal. Whatever their use, they allow ordinary people to make things quickly, cheaply, and easily.

For example, a 3-D printer could create a missing part for your bicycle or build you a unique keychain—and all you need to do is download the design. 3-D printers also mean that more people can be entrepreneurs. If you can design a big idea on a computer, you can print it at home to sell. Or you can sell your idea online to others who can print it.

INSPIRING STORIES

3-D Printing

In 2014, the Toronto Public Library began to offer 3-D printers at some branches. 3-D printers are becoming cheaper, but they are still too expensive for most people to own. People can now send their designs to the library for printing. Thanks to libraries and private companies, there are now more than 20,000 public 3-D printing centers around the world.

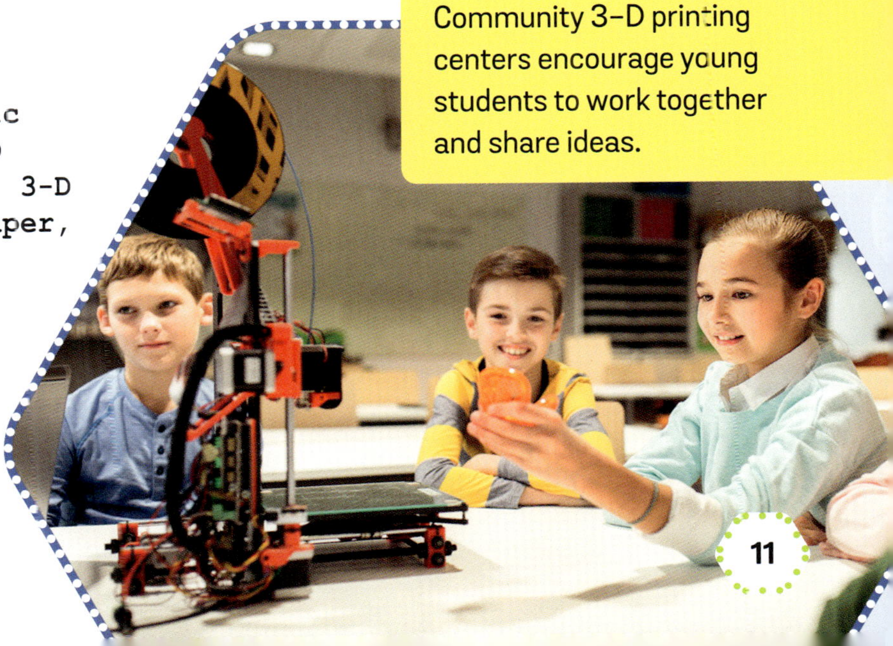

Community 3-D printing centers encourage young students to work together and share ideas.

3-D START-UP STARS:

BRAM DE ZWART AND BRIAN GARRETT

After completing a Master of Science degree at the Delft University of Technology in the Netherlands, Bram de Zwart worked as a product manager for 3D Systems. The company sells 3-D printers and other products. There, he met designer Brian Garrett, who had graduated from the Eindhoven University of Technology. The two men realized that, for many people, 3-D printers were too expensive to buy for the printing they wanted to do. They thought that 3-D printers would be used more often if people who wanted to use them could connect with 3-D printer owners.

De Zwart and Garrett saw a need that was not being met—to make 3-D printing available to many more people. They talked to the owners of 3-D printers and asked if they would be willing to print off designs from other people for a fee. Lots of owners agreed, and the two entrepreneurs left 3D Systems in 2013 to set up their own start-up company, 3D Hubs.

3D Systems, where de Zwart and Garrett worked, was one of the first companies to sell 3-D printers.

MAKING 3-D BIG

3D Hubs use an Internet platform to connect individual designers with nearby printers. De Zwart and Garrett designed software that people could use to upload their designs. The software checks for mistakes, and **estimates** the printing costs.

The entrepreneurs also created **partnerships** with 3-D printer owners who could print designs for people to pick up. Within a year of setting up their company, de Zwart and Garrett had 7,000 locations in 140 countries where people could pick up their printing. There are now even more locations.

3D HUBS

3D Hubs' network of 3-D printer owners are paid for what they print.

SMALL PRINTERS, BIG CHANGES

For Bram de Zwart, 3-D printers dramatically and positively change the way that things are made. People can simply print what they need at home. They no longer have to rely on large factories that produce lots of goods and ship them around the world. This means less waste and less pollution. In de Zwart's words, "We can eventually change how products are being made and **distributed**. You can make products both local and on demand."

By providing software to 3-D printer owners, 3D Hubs can more quickly expand its business around the world.

TINY TECHNOLOGY

Small things can make big changes. The idea of tiny technology, called **nanotechnology**, began with the American **physicist** Richard Feynman. In 1959, he figured out that it was possible to move **atoms** and change **molecules** to make things. Everything on Earth—including us—is made of atoms and molecules. Working with atoms and molecules makes it possible to create almost anything!

WORKING AT A SMALL SCALE

In 1981, two researchers working for the computer company IBM created the scanning tunneling microscope (STM). The STM allowed them to see things at an atomic level. This means that they could see the individual atoms that make up something.

The first molecular motor was made in 1999 by Dr. T. Ross Kelly of Boston College. He believed that these motors would make micro-robots possible in the future. Micro-robots could move around small spaces doing big jobs. They could build or repair anything, from organs in the human body to the walls of buildings.

Events such as RoboCup encourage people, including students, to get involved in science-related challenges.

A cable just 0.04 inches (1 mm) thick that is made of carbon nanotubes can withstand up to 14,110 pounds (6,400 kg) of weight.

MICRO MATERIALS

Nanotechnology is about more than just micro-robots. Building from molecules helps us make objects that are extra strong or work in special ways. Nanotubes are a good example of nanotechnology in industry. These are tubes of **carbon** atoms that are thinner than a human hair, but stronger than steel! They are used to create many different goods, from sports equipment to cars.

SHARK TECHNOLOGY

In 2002, Dr. Tony Brennan wondered why sharks were never covered in algae. He looked closely at shark skin and saw it was made up of tiny diamond-shaped cells covered in millions of small ridges. These ridges stop the algae from growing. Dr. Brennan created a plastic material called Sharklet that reproduced the shark cells' pattern. Sharklet prevents the growth of bacteria. In 2007, Dr. Brennan worked with entrepreneur Mark Spiecker to manufacture this plastic. It is used in hospitals to stop the spread of some types of germs.

INSPIRING STORIES

RoboCup

The first RoboCup was held in Osaka, Japan, in November 1996. Eight robot soccer teams competed against each other. The robots were not nanotech, but getting a team of independent robots to work together toward a common goal is one of the main challenges of nanotechnology. Robotics challenges such as RoboCup invite teams of universities, businesses, and small start-ups to compete. They also help develop research into artificial intelligence (AI).

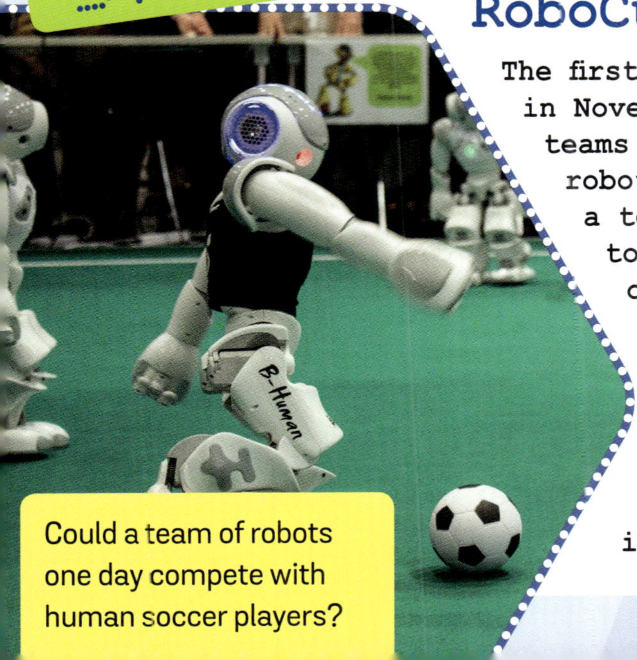

Could a team of robots one day compete with human soccer players?

NANOTECH START-UP STAR: RACHEL PAUTLER

In 2014, Rachel Pautler was an engineering student at a University of Waterloo program in nanotechnology. She was doing research, and while the research was cutting edge, she was not satisfied with the results. All she had were research papers, and no sense that she was changing the world in a significant way.

That changed when she looked into start-ups. Waterloo, Ontario, is known for its many start-up companies in the high-tech industry. Pautler needed a product, and she and her fellow students Andrew Martinko, Derek Jouppi, and Chad Sweeting found it. They were researching how particular molecules reacted to certain types of light. From this, they created an ink made of molecules that changed color under UV rays from the Sun. The ink becomes invisible when sunscreen is applied over it. When the sunscreen wears off, the ink reappears. This tells the wearer it is time to apply more sunscreen. Pautler's professor told her that she and her classmates should start up a company to sell it.

The rays from the Sun can be very dangerous. Protecting against them is big business!

REACHING THE MARKET

Pautler and her partners formed Suncayr to look at ways to use the ink as a product they could sell. The company developed a marker that could write the special ink on skin. They also made stickers printed with this ink that could be stuck directly on the skin. They worked with doctors specializing in skin and child health, who tested the product to make sure it was safe. For Pautler, turning her nanotech studies into a product to sell meant that she had gone beyond research. She had moved on to making something that could change the world, even if only by making sure people better protected their skin against sunburn and skin cancer.

NEW CHALLENGES

Suncayr continues to develop its special ink and is bringing it to the market. Pautler has left the company. She is now working as a director of sales and marketing in another company. However, her experiences at school and at her first company stay with her as she moves on to her next challenges. For Pautler, being an entrepreneur does not stop with a single idea or a single product. Each step she takes stays with her as she learns from what she has done. She then applies it to new ideas and new business opportunities.

In 2014, Pautler and her partners at Suncayr were the only Canadian nominees for a prestigious award celebrating the best inventions designed by university students.

WE HAVE THE POWER!

Factories and businesses cannot work without power. Burning fossil fuels to make the electricity that industries need adds greenhouse gases to our atmosphere and contributes to climate change. Our current **power grid** is becoming older and less effective. Fortunately, entrepreneurs are looking at new ways to **generate** and distribute power.

RENEWABLE START-UPS

Entrepreneurs have established a number of companies to produce and sell renewable energy. Instead of burning fossil fuels, renewable energy creates power from renewable sources, such as the Sun's rays or wind. Many companies make **wind turbines**—windmills that can generate power from wind. Other companies set up **solar panels**. In 2007, Azeem M. Qureshi helped establish Grasshopper Solar. This company pays people and businesses to install solar panels on the roofs of their homes and buildings. These panels feed power into the power grid. The building owners are paid to produce renewable energy.

Villages in communities that do not have electricity could install solar panels to generate affordable power.

There are also entrepreneurs who are trying to improve the way the existing power grid works. In 2016, Jordan Kennie, Daniel Larsen, and Erik Hatfield set up Stash Energy Storage. The company sells a heat pump, which generates and stores energy at night. This saves money, because electricity is cheaper at night when fewer people are using it. The stored energy can be used to provide electricity during times of the day when more people are using it—and prices are higher. This saves people money and helps the electrical grid work more effectively.

Solar power works well in places located around the equator. There is more sunshine there, allowing solar panels to generate a lot of electricity.

SMALL IS BEAUTIFUL

In some parts of the world, there is no power grid. This means that many people do not have electricity. However, entrepreneurs are also working to provide power to these communities. Villages, schools, and hospitals can generate reliable, cheap power using solar panels or small hydroelectric power plants. Small-scale, renewable power plants are cheaper and much better for the environment.

INSPIRING STORIES

Power for Everyone

Canadian Jason Gray and business partner Andy Moon established SunFarmer in 2012. This organization helps entrepreneurs around the world set up small-scale solar power projects to power schools and hospitals. The projects provide reliable power in places with no electrical grid. Gray and Moon want to provide electricity to the 1.2 billion people around the world who do not have access to it. They want to empower local entrepreneurs in these communities. That way, they can ensure that solar power is available to those who need it.

SunFarmer installed solar panels at the Bayalpata Hospital in Nepal.

ELECTRIC START-UP STAR: ELENA FOUKES LUCAS

Elena Foukes Lucas began her career at Pacific Gas and Electric Company (PG&E). She had a passion for promoting renewable and **green energy**. Some of her early projects were on energy efficiency programs for low-income people. She helped set up small-scale power plants close to where people who use the power live and work. Working for a big company, however, meant that some of her ideas did not get approved by the departments she worked for. This made her frustrated, and she decided to form her own business. In 2014, at the age of 25, Lucas left PG&E and helped set up UtilityAPI. This company makes it easier for homeowners and businesses to see how much energy they are using. Previously, it was difficult to get data from power companies. UtilityAPI made it easier through software, so green energy companies could help homeowners and business owners see if green energy was right for them. The software can show if green energy could save people money.

Elena Lucas is passionate about helping people make the best choices about energy use.

MAKING BETTER DECISIONS

UtilityAPI helps green energy companies show potential customers how much energy they use, how that energy is produced, and whether they could use more green energy instead. This way, people can make better choices, use less energy, and burn less fossil fuels that contribute to climate change.

TOP ENTREPRENEUR

In 2016, *Forbes* magazine named Lucas as one of their top 30 entrepreneurs under the age of 30. This list celebrates young entrepreneurs who have done impressive things in business early in their lives.

ADVICE FOR YOUNG ENTREPRENEURS

Lucas is the CEO of UtilityAPI. She also speaks about her experiences in promoting green energy and how to help women become technology entrepreneurs. Lucas encourages people to start from the top through their own company, instead of starting from the bottom rung of a big company and working their way to the top. By attending entrepreneur and start-up events and meeting interesting people, young would-be entrepreneurs can find help from other entrepreneurs. They can then get started working on their own big ideas.

Many people want their electricity to come from renewable sources such as solar and wind power. UtilityAPI helps them make informed decisions about energy.

COMPUTERS AND ROBOTS

Ever since people invented machines, they have imagined having robots smart enough to take orders and do our work for us. That dream is now a reality.

In 1943, British engineer Thomas Flowers helped invent Colossus, the world's first electronic computer that could be programmed. This early computer was huge and filled an entire room! It was used by Alan Turing to break the German Enigma codes during World War II. The first robot that could be programmed was Unimate, which was invented in 1961 by American George Devol. He sold it to General Motors, where it was used to lift and stack hot metal parts. After that, computers and robots became smaller, faster, and more capable.

COMPUTER START-UPS

By the 1970s, computers had become smaller and affordable enough for most people to own. Soon, computer entrepreneurship took off. You may have an Apple computer or iPhone thanks to the work started by Steve Jobs and Steve Wozniak in a California garage. You may use software designed by Bill Gates, who established Microsoft in 1975 when he was just 20. You could be searching the Internet thanks to Larry Page and Sergey Brin, who created Google while they were students at Stanford University in California.

These people not only invented computer hardware and software, but they also inspired other entrepreneurs. Around the world, hundreds of young entrepreneurs are now setting up companies designing software or hardware. They are hoping to be the next Bill Gates or Steve Jobs.

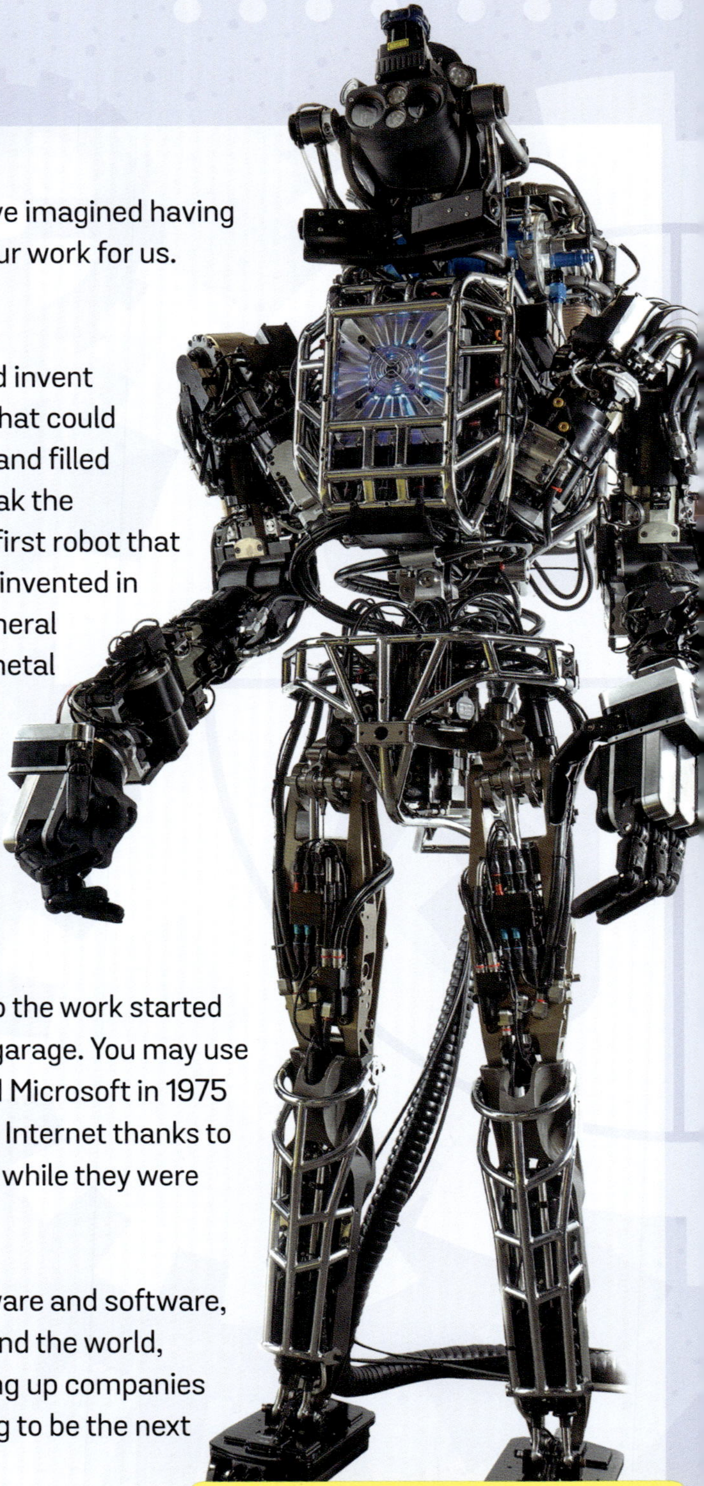

Innovations in robotics are one of the most exciting areas of science and technology start-ups.

Sergey Brin and Larry Page founded Google, which now includes projects such as self-driving cars and deliveries by drone.

THE FUTURE IS NOW

Computers are now in phones and in wristwatches. They may someday be part of our bodies, helping us see, sending us information, even translating languages.

Someday, robots may enter our bodies to heal and repair us during illness or after accidents. The technology already exists for most of this to happen, and it will only get easier as time goes on.

INSPIRING STORIES

The Stemettes

The Stemettes is a group created by British math **prodigy** Anne-Marie Imafidon in 2013. It encourages young women to study science, technology, engineering, and mathematics (STEM). The Stemettes organize events at which women in STEM-related industries meet and talk to young female STEM fans. The organization also created the Outbox Incubator. The incubator—a word that refers to a place where things grow—helps young female entrepreneurs launch STEM-related businesses. The incubator also provides funding for particularly good business ideas.

The Stemettes help young women gain confidence to pursue their ideas as entrepreneurs.

ROBOTIC START-UP STAR:

MARC RAIBERT

From when he was a student, Marc Raibert was fascinated by how robots could move. After getting his Ph.D. at the Massachusetts Institute of Technology (MIT), he became a professor of electrical engineering and computer science at the university. There, he helped set up a robotics engineering laboratory called the Leg Lab. The Leg Lab aimed to create robots that had functional, or working, legs. Raibert challenged himself to find a way to make a robot figure out how to balance itself, so it would not fall over when it walked. To do this, he invented a robot with one leg. The One-Leg Hopper was designed with sensors and a computer. These could measure and keep the robot's balance as it bounced on its one leg. By mastering balance, Raibert could apply what he learned to robots that moved on four legs or on two legs.

BigDog (see opposite) is designed to help soldiers by carrying their gear over rough ground.

DYNAMIC THINKING

Raibert was 43 when he started Boston Dynamics. Building from his research at MIT, he created a company to build robots. These robots could pick up heavy loads and walk over uneven ground. One of his methods was to look at how animals in nature handled walking. He copied those designs for his robots.

In 2005, Boston Dynamics built BigDog. This machine has four legs bent in a way that make it look like a dog. It was designed to follow soldiers over ground that was too rough for vehicles. It could carry 340 pounds (154 kg) at 4 miles (6.4 km) per hour. In 2012, Boston Dynamics created the Cheetah, a four-legged robot that could run at speeds of 20 miles (32 km) per hour. In 2016, they unveiled Atlas, a two-legged robot that walked like a person. It could walk over icy ground and quickly pick itself up if it fell.

WORKERS OF THE FUTURE?

Marc Raibert continues to work as president and project manager at Boston Dynamics. He hopes that his robots will help carry things for soldiers on missions, or help search-and-rescue workers. Robots such as Atlas can look for people in collapsed buildings and other places too dangerous for humans to go. They could also be used to do simple tasks at warehouses and factories, carrying and lifting crates, and making things.

Marc Raibert continues to explore and experiment. Walking robots are part of his lifelong passion.

ENTREPRENEURS CHANGING THE WORLD

Not so long ago, the world was a different place. Most people worked on farms, and most goods were made close to where they lived. But our understanding of science changed all this. New discoveries such as the steam engine and electricity helped us create goods in great quantities and ship them around the world. Now, computers allow today's entrepreneurs to instantly reach buyers and sellers around the world.

However, the change in our understanding of science is only part of the picture—it was entrepreneurs who made the difference. They had the ideas and saw the opportunities to turn them into reality. They made the investments to build factories, railroads, and Internet connections. They made the goods and started selling them. Thanks to entrepreneurs, in just a few decades, most people's lives became easier and healthier.

A science and technology education emphasizes critical thinking and teamwork. Sharing ideas and learning from others is important.

Playing with your designs is a key part of innovation and discovery. This young designer uses Lego blocks to build and adapt his computer design.

FUTURE CHALLENGES AND OPPORTUNITIES

The changes of the Industrial Revolution were not without problems. We are still facing some of these problems today, such as pollution and climate change. However, these challenges also present opportunities for entrepreneurs. There is an increasing demand for renewable energy to replace fossil fuels. Some industrial jobs have disappeared as technologies have changed. However, new, exciting roles for engineers working with computers, robots, and other new technologies are springing up. Things that could once only be made in big factories can now be made in your home or with a visit to a local library or 3-D printing hub.

START-UPS ARE THE FUTURE

Think of the changes that have happened since the beginning of the 1800s thanks to innovative inventions. Imagine how different things will be after the next 50 years. Will electric self-driving cars meet us at our door as we go to work? Will we have to go to work if we can make goods and provide services at home? Will our homes be powerhouses with a wind turbine in our backyard or solar panels on our roofs? Whatever the future holds, it will be shaped by brilliant young entrepreneurs—and perhaps you will be one of them!

YOUR START-UP STORY

We have learned how entrepreneurs working in science and technology have changed our world. We have also learned about the industries they have shaped, and the challenges that have sparked their ideas.

TAKE THE START-UP CHALLENGE!

One of the challenges we have to overcome in the near future is our reliance on fossil fuels. We need to switch over to renewable energy sources and avoid wasting energy where we live and work. How can you use what you have learned as an entrepreneur to handle this challenge?

Remember that entrepreneurs have ideas that they can develop to sell to the public. They research an idea, looking at ways to solve a problem or meet a need. To succeed as an entrepreneur, choose a field or activity that you enjoy. Then think about where you can research more about the topic. Figure out ways you can use your research to help people, and how you might convince them to support your ideas or business. Why not try the activity on the next page to kick off your entrepreneur career?

Experimenting is an important learning tool. Observe what happens while you experiment, and write down your findings.

START-UP CHALLENGE

TRY OUT AN ENERGY AUDIT

An energy **audit** of a home helps homeowners learn how much energy they are using. It suggests ways they can reduce energy usage or switch to renewable options. Wasted energy costs money and contributes to global climate change. Research things to look for around your home that might indicate that energy is being wasted. Some suggestions are below.

- Locate air leaks by examining drafts around windows, doors, and other areas.
- Check your home's **insulation** to make sure there is enough and that it is keeping heat in. Online sources can help you determine where and how to look.
- Check your home's lighting. What kind of light bulbs are being used?
- Check how old and energy **efficient** your **appliances** are.

Find three ways that you can improve the energy usage in your home, so that you use less, waste less, or use renewable energy. Use these questions to guide you.

- How much money does your family spend per month on energy?
- Are there ways to use less energy in your home?
- Can you install alternative energy sources in your home, such as solar panels on the roof?
- How much money would it cost to put your solution into action? How much money per month would it save? How long would it take for the energy solution to pay for itself?

Tesla's cars promise to change the way we drive. What will your innovation change?

GLOSSARY

air resistance The way air pushes against something that is moving through it. The faster the object moves through the air, the greater the resistance.
appliances Machines that do work in your house, such as refrigerators, stoves, and dishwashers
atoms Tiny parts of a substance
audit An investigation
carbon A particular atom that is found in things such as carbon nanotubes, carbon dioxide, and oil and gas
CEO (short for **Chief Executive Officer**) A person who is in charge of a company
computer-aided designs Computer programs used to create precise technical drawings or illustrations
distributed Gave something out to people who use it
efficient Achieving something using less energy or doing less work
electric car A car that runs only on energy stored its rechargeable batteries
entrepreneur A person who creates a business and takes on most of the risk to operate it
estimates Makes a rough guess about the size or amount of something
factory A building or complex where workers and machines make goods in large quantities
fossil fuels Nonrenewable fuels made from oil or natural gas, found deep underground, made from the remains of plants and animals that lived millions of years ago
fuel Material such as oil, wood, or gasoline that is burned to produce heat or energy
generate To create or produce something
global warming Heating of Earth's atmosphere caused by increased levels of carbon dioxide and other pollutants
goods Products; something made
green energy Energy that is produced from sources that do not pollute, such as solar power and wind power
greenhouse gas emissions Gases, such as carbon dioxide or methane, which trap the Sun's heat within Earth's atmosphere, warming the planet
Industrial Revolution A period of time around the 1800s in Europe and America in which machines were invented that could do the work of many people
industry Business activities concerned with the processing of raw materials and the manufacturing of goods in factories
innovative Describing something that no one else has done before
insulation Something that blocks the movement, transfer, or leakage of heat and cold
invested Gave money to help start up a company in exchange for owning part of that company
locomotive A vehicle that runs on rails and pulls other cars
manufacturing The process of making goods to sell
molecules Groups of atoms bonded together
nanotechnology The science of making things work at the molecular level
network A system of things that are connected together, such as computers on the Internet
orbit The curved path a space object or spacecraft travels around a star, planet, or moon
partnerships Teams of two people who work together toward a common goal
physicist A scientist who studies or specializes in physics, which is the science dealing with the nature and properties of matter and energy
power grid The system of wires that brings electricity from power plants to homes and buildings
prodigy Someone, especially somebody young, who is unusually good at something
remote Far from anything else

satellites Objects that orbit planets

services Types of help or work that someone does for someone else

shingles Materials placed on a roof to protect it from rain and snow

software Programs and operating information that are used by a computer to do something

solar panels Devices that generate electricity from sunlight

solar-powered Using energy from the Sun to do work, such as create electricity

space tourism Visiting space from Earth

steam power Using steam to do work, such as pushing a generator to create electricity, or moving the wheels of a steam locomotive

ultraviolet (UV) light Invisible light beyond the violet end of the color spectrum

wind turbines Power plants that generate energy from the wind, such as windmills

LEARNING MORE

BOOKS

Cameron, Schyrlet, and Carolyn Craig. *STEM Labs for Middle Grades*. Mark Twain Media, 2016.

Cornell, Kari. *Facebook Founder and Internet Entrepreneur: Mark Zuckerberg*. Lerner Publications, 2016.

Doeden, Matt. *SpaceX and Tesla Motors Engineer: Elon Musk*. Lerner Publications, 2015.

Eliot, Matthew. *Kid Millionaire: Over 100 Exciting Business Ideas*. Sterling Publishing Co Inc., 2016.

Toren, Adam, and Matthew Toren. *Kidpreneur$: Young Entrepreneurs with Big Ideas!* Business Plus Media Group, 2009.

WEBSITES

Teaching Kids Business

https://teachingkidsbusiness.com

This site offers resources for youth, parents, and teachers about how to set up and run businesses.

BizKids

http://bizkids.com

A website teaching youth how to watch their money and handle business. Features videos, lesson plans, games, and a blog.

Engineering: Go For It!

www.egfi-k12.org

An engineering site for youth. Offers career advice and entertaining information on the fields of engineering.

Teen Business

www.teenbusiness.com

A support site for teens showing other teens who have set up their own business. Features profiles, videos, and advice.

INDEX

3-D printing 10–13, 27
3D Hubs 12–13
3D Systems 10, 12

Apple 22

battery wall 9
BigDog 24, 25
Boston Dynamics 25
Brennan, Dr. Tony 15
Brin, Sergey 22, 23

cars 4–9, 10, 15, 23, 27, 29
cell phones 22, 23
Classic Factory 6
computers 8, 10, 11, 14, 22–23, 24, 26, 27

de Zwart, Bram 12–13

electric cars 4, 6–7, 8, 27
Elextra electric car 6
energy audit 29
energy storage 9, 19
experimenting 5, 25, 28

Feynman, Richard 14
Flowers, Thomas 22
fossil fuels 6, 9, 17, 18, 21, 28

Garrett, Brian 12–13
Gates, Bill 22
Google 22, 23
Grasshopper Solar 18
Gray, Jason 19
green energy 20–21
greenhouse gas emissions 6, 18

Hull, Chuck 10
Hyperloop 9

IBM 14

Jobs, Steve 22

Kelly, Dr. T. Ross 14

Leg Lab 24
Lucas, Elena Foukes 20–21

micro-robots 14
Microsoft 22
molecular robots 14
monitoring electricity use 20–21
Moon, Andy 19
Musk, Elon 4, 5, 7, 8–9

nanotechnology 14, 15
nanotubes 15

One-Leg Hopper 24

Page, Larry 22, 23
Pautler, Rachel 16–17
PayPal 8
pollution reduction 6, 13

Qureshi, Azeem M. 18

Raibert, Marc 24–25
renewable energy sources 18–19, 20–21, 27
RoboCup 14, 15
robots 9, 14–15, 22, 23, 24–25

satellites 9
scanning tunneling microscope (STM) 14
self-driving cars 9, 27
Sharklet 15
Shen, Freeman 7
solar power 7, 9, 18, 19, 21, 27, 29
solar-powered car 7
space tourism 9
SpaceX 9
Spiecker, Mark 15
start-up challenge 28–29
Stash Energy Storage 19
steam engines 5, 26
STEM 23
Stemettes 23
Stephenson, George 5
Suncayr 16–17
SunFarmer 19
sunscreen 16–17

Tesla, Nikola 7
Tesla Motors 4, 7, 29
trains 5, 9
Turing, Alan 22

Unimate robot 22
UtilityAPI 20–21

waste reduction 13
WEY hybrid car 7
Wi-Fi network 9
wind power 18, 21, 27
WM Motors 7

Zip2 8

ABOUT THE AUTHOR

James Bow is the author of more than 40 educational books for children and young adults. He is also a novelist and a columnist, and holds a degree in Urban and Regional Planning.